MYSTERIES IN HISTORY

What Was Stonehenge For?

Solving the Mysteries of the Past

Anita Croy

Cavendish Square
New York

Published in 2018 by Cavendish Square Publishing, LLC
243 5th Avenue, Suite 136 New York, NY 10016

Website: cavendishsq.com

© 2018 Brown Bear Books Ltd

Cataloging-in-Publication Data

Names: Croy, Anita.
Title: What was Stonehenge for? / Anita Croy.
Description: New York : Cavendish Square Publishing, 2018. | Series: Mysteries in history: solving the mysteries of the past | Includes index.
Identifiers: ISBN 9781502627940 (library bound) | ISBN 9781502627957 (ebook)
Subjects: LCSH: Megalithic monuments--England--Juvenile literature. | Stonehenge (England)--Juvenile literature. | England--Antiquities--Juvenile literature.
Classification: LCC DA142.C35 2018 | DDC 936.2/319--dc23

For Brown Bear Books Ltd:
Managing Editor: Tim Cooke
Designer: Lynne Lennon
Design Manager: Keith Davis
Editorial Director: Lindsey Lowe
Children's Publisher: Anne O'Daly
Picture Manager: Sophie Mortimer

Picture Credits:
Front Cover: Mavratti/Wikimedia Commons
Interior: Alamy: Skyscan Photolibrary 29; **Atlas van Loon:** 14; **Curios Ireland:** 19; **Dreamstime:** Grafvision 24, Martin Srubar 15; **English Heritage:** 18; **GFDL:** 21; **Public Domain:** Adamscan 9, Miguel Hermoso Cuesta 17, Joseph Lertola 13, Psychosteveuk 43; **Rex Features:** Associated Press 4cl; **Robert Hunt Library:** 23, 32; **Rock World:** 27tl; **Shutterstock:** 1000 Words 16, Stephane Bidouze 39, Frank Zack 20, Jaroslava V12, 36, Teo Nuvoli 40-41, Peter David Robinson 35; **Thinkstock:** istockphoto 1, 4/5, 6/7, 7r. 8, 10, 11, 22, 25, 26-27, 28, 30, 31, 33, 34, 37, 38, 40t, 44, 45; **West Lothian Archaeology:** Dr John Wells 42.

Brown Bear Books has made every attempt to contact the copyright holder.
If you have any information please contact licensing@brownbearbooks.co.uk

All websites were available and accurate when this book went to press.

Manufactured in the United States of America

CPSIA compliance information: Batch #CS17CSQ.

Contents

What Is Stonehenge?...........................4

Who Built Stonehenge?......................14

How Was Stonehenge Built?...............24

Why Did People Build Stone Circles?...36

Glossary..46

Further Resources 47

Index 48

What Is Stonehenge?

The huge stone circle of Stonehenge in southwest England is one of the most well-known monuments of the prehistoric world. But why was it built?

A modern-day **druid** celebrates the summer solstice at Stonehenge.

Every year people gather at Stonehenge to watch the sun rise on the summer **solstice**, the longest day of the year. They believe the stones were erected as a kind of calendar. They think the farmers who built the monument used it to follow the movement of the stars in the sky throughout the year.

The movements of the stars told them when it was the right time to plant their crops or when to hold special **rituals**. **Archaeologists** do not know if this is true. There are many **theories** about the purpose of Stonehenge. No one knows which is correct.

Preseli Hills

Stonehenge

IN CONTEXT

Salisbury Plain
Stonehenge stands on Salisbury Plain, a **plateau** that covers about 300 square miles (780 sq km). The grassy plain is home to many early buildings. As well as Stonehenge, early people built burial mounds called barrows, stone circles, and **earthworks**, such as Durrington Walls, on the plain. Much later, in the 500s BCE, Iron Age peoples built hilltop forts there.

Only parts of the monument still stand upright. Other stones have fallen down over thousands of years.

How and Who?

In many ways, Stonehenge does not seem mysterious. The stone circle is huge. It can be seen from miles away. But the monument's size does not make it easier to understand. Experts have studied Stonehenge for centuries. They have found out a lot about how it was built. They have learned about the farming people who built it on the plain outside the modern town of Salisbury. Today, archaeologists use the most up-to-date techniques to analyze the monument. They hope that learning more about the stone circle will reveal more about why it was built.

Could It Be True?

What are other theories about Stonehenge? One of the strangest ideas is that it was built by people from the lost city of Atlantis.

The huge statues on Easter Island were thought to have been built by aliens.

Atlantis was a legendary ancient city that was said to have disappeared beneath the ocean. To date, there is no evidence that Atlantis ever existed. Another theory is that Stonehenge was a landing site for alien aircraft. The pyramids in Giza, Egypt, and the statues of Easter Island in the Pacific Ocean were also said to be the work of aliens.

What's In a Name?

The name "Stonehenge" means "hanging stones" in the language of the Saxons. The Saxons were some of the earliest inhabitants of Britain.

The "hanging stones" are the flat stones across the top of the upright stones.

7

ANCIENT SECRETS

How old is it?

Radiocarbon dating was developed in the 1960s. It helped experts to be much more accurate in dating objects. All organic, or living, objects contain **carbon**. After they die, the carbon decays. Scientists can date how old a tree, person, or animal is by how much carbon has decayed. At Stonehenge, scientists dated animal and human bones they found buried close to the stones. The results gave them the dates experts use today for the site.

The name refers to the large flat stones, which today are called lintels, that lie on top of a horseshoe-shape of **standing stones** in the center of Stonehenge. The flat stones "hang" in the air. These central stones are what people usually picture when they think of Stonehenge. In fact, they are just one part of the story of a much larger site.

The Saxons named the site in the 400s CE, but does that mean they also built it? In the 1960s, new dating

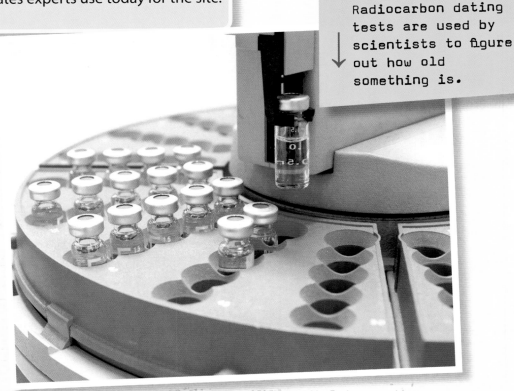

Radiocarbon dating tests are used by scientists to figure out how old something is.

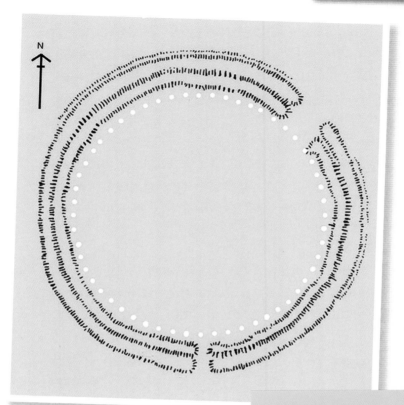

N

The first monument was a circular ditch. The white marks are holes that were dug and then filled back in.

techniques were used on animal bones found near the stones. Bones of different ages revealed that Stonehenge had been built in three separate stages. Construction took thousands of years, from around 3100 BCE to around 1100 BCE.

What Came First?

Around 5,000 years ago, the earliest builders at Stonehenge used tools made from deer antlers to dig a large, circular ditch. The ditch surrounded a very large enclosure with two entrances. From the air, the shape of the ditch can still be clearly seen today.

Experts believe the builders used the chalky earth they had dug up to create a bank around the ditch. They dug lots of small holes into the bank, but then filled them back in. No one knows what these holes were for. Experts have dated the antler tools found at the site to around 3100 BCE.

The circular ditch and bank are known as Stonehenge I. Bones suggest that the site was used for about 500 years before it was abandoned. But what was it used for, and why was it abandoned?

Stonehenge II

In about 2100 BCE, about 1,000 years after Stonehenge I was created, a second version of the monument was built. This time, the builders set up around 80 tall, thin **volcanic** rocks in two circles, one inside the other, in the center of the monument. The rocks are known as bluestones, because they turn blue when they are wet. Both stone circles had an entrance that faced toward sunrise on Midsummer's Day, the summer solstice.

←
The builders of Stonehenge I used deer antlers as tools to dig the circular ditch.

↑ The Chacoan people carved the sun spiral high on Fajada Butte.

Stonehenge III

One hundred years later, builders removed the bluestones. They put up structures using huge blocks of a kind of sandstone called sarsen. They erected a circle of sarsen stones joined by lintels to form a continuous circular band. They built a horseshoe of five sarsen arches inside the circle.

However, archaeologists discovered that, over the next 500 years, the position of the stones at Stonehenge was changed yet again.

ANCIENT SECRETS

Summer Solstice

In the past, many peoples believed the summer solstice had a special **spiritual** meaning. The Chacoan people of New Mexico carved a spiral into a rock high on an outcrop named Fajada Butte. It is carefully positioned so that, on the summer solstice, a sharp dagger of sunlight cuts precisely across the center of the spiral. No one knows how the Chacoan were able to create this special marker—or what they might have used it for.

↑ The stones line up with the sunrise on the summer and winter solstices.

Scientists discovered that builders had added a circle of bluestones inside the circle of sarsens, and a horseshoe of bluestone inside the horseshoe of sarsens. The tallest of the bluestones lined up with sunrise on the summer solstice. It is called the "altar stone," but no one knows if it was ever used as an altar. Other individual stones also have names. The "heel stone" marks the entrance. Nearby is the horizontal "slaughter stone." Despite its name, experts do not think it was used for **sacrifices**. It is probably lying flat because it fell over.

When was Stonehenge finally completed? Experts think that the monument we see today dates from around 1100 BCE. Builders had widened the entrance and created a path to connect the stones with the Avon River nearby.

Changing Appearance

Stonehenge has changed over many years. Much of the site is in ruins. Many of the stones have fallen down. Other stones have been taken from the site. But the different stages of building all left traces for experts to study. For example, archaeologists now believe that a wooden structure stood at the monument during the period of Stonehenge II. Tests on the soil show where timber posts were once dug into the earth.

SCIENCE SOLVES IT

Reconstruction

The arrows on this digital reconstruction of Stonhenge show the direction of sunrise (A) and sunset (B) on the summer solstice (*top right and top left*), and sunrise (C) and sunset (D) on the winter solstice (*bottom right and bottom left*).

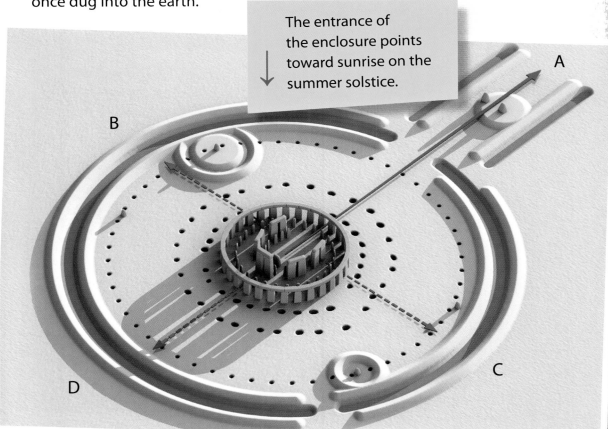

The entrance of the enclosure points toward sunrise on the summer solstice.

B

A

D

C

Who Built Stonehenge?

There are many different theories about who built Stonehenge. Will it ever be known for certain who raised the monument?

In the past, archaeologists have suggested at various times that the ancient Celts, the ancient Romans, and the ancient Egyptians might have built Stonehenge. The Celts were a European people who settled in Britain in about 750 BCE.

This is a drawing of the monument from the 1800s.

The Romans invaded Britain in 55 BCE. The ancient Egyptians, however, had never even been in Britain. The only reason some people thought the Egyptians might have built Stonehenge was because they built the pyramids.

An Easy Mistake?

In the 1800s the English archaeologist John Aubrey was one of the first people to study Stonehenge carefully. He decided that the Celts must have built it. How did he reach this conclusion? Aubrey had visited stone circles in Scotland and Ireland. He knew that, after the Romans invaded Britain, the Celts had fled to Scotland and Ireland. He therefore assumed that all stone circles must be the work of the Celts.

A modern-day
druid visits
Stonehenge for
the summer
solstice.

Aubrey suggested that Stonehenge was a
temple for the Celtic priests called druids. His
theory was very popular. For centuries, people
believed that Stonehenge was a **ceremonial** center for the druids.
People dressed as druids still gather at Stonehenge to celebrate
sunrise on Midsummer's Day.

In the 1960s, when scientists began to use a new method
called radiocarbon dating on bone tools and traces of wood at
Stonehenge, they discovered that the monument was far older
than they had thought. By the time the Celts had even arrived
in Britain, Stonehenge was nearly 3,000 years old.

A Long Construction

Experts now know that the first monument was built near the end of the New Stone Age or Neolithic Age. This was a period of history that lasted from around 7000 to 2000 BCE. Over 5,000 years, early humans changed from being hunter-gatherers to people who lived in villages, learned how to grow crops, and raised livestock.

IN CONTEXT

Early Farmers
Experts now know that farming began in West Asia and spread to Europe. The arrival of farming brought other changes. It helped create trading networks among peoples that led to the swapping of ideas and what we now call technology. Because early people did not have to spend all their time finding food, they perhaps had more time for other activities, such as constructing stone monuments.

This reconstruction shows how early people were often buried with their possessions.

A Sacred Site?

These early Neolithic farmers seem to have developed a **belief system** that was linked to the landscape. They began to use earthworks to mark sites in the landscape that they believed were particularly important. This is probably why they built the original ditch and bank at Stonehenge I.

Were the builders of Stonehenge the first to build such a circle? Accurate dating methods suggest that they were not. The earliest **enclosures** in Britain date from about 4000 BCE. They are about 1,000 years older than Stonehenge. Windmill Hill nearby was built in around 3675 BCE.

Similar circular ditches and mounds have been found at Windmill Hill.

The Beaker People are named for the drinking vessels they made.

IN CONTEXT

Telling the Difference

Experts use specific clues to try to tell apart the peoples who lived on Salisbury Plain at different times. The Windmill Hill People built the first earth circles on the plain. The Beaker People who followed them were probably newcomers to Britain. They buried their dead in graves with pottery cups shaped like an upside-down bell. The later Wessex People used bronze weapons and built stone tombs covered with earth mounds. Whether these groups were related to one another is not known.

The Windmill Hill People

The people who built circular trenches and mounds at Windmill Hill, a site close to Stonehenge, are named the Windmill Hill People. Experts have learned that these people came from eastern England and were among the first people to settle in the southwest. They lived a **semi-nomadic** life as they hunted animals and gathered fruit and berries for food. Many animal bones have been found at Windmill Hill. They buried their dead together in large stone-lined tombs that faced east to west. The earthworks were built using circular and **symmetrical** designs. It is thought that the Windmill Hill People believed such patterns had a spiritual meaning.

IN CONTEXT

Sacred Landscapes

Europe's stone monuments were part of a landscape of **sacred** hills, lakes, rivers, mountains, and trees. The structures often lay at the heart of a sacred site. Later peoples also built monumental structures. In North America, the Hopewell of the Ohio Valley marked their graves with large mounds after about 200 CE. Later, the Mississippian Culture (1000–1450 CE) held ceremonies to mark the summer and winter solstices. They built temples on top of large earthen mounds.

↑ This Hopewell site in Ohio is home to a number of earthen mounds.

Who came next?

The next group to settle in the area near Stonehenge were the Beaker People. These people probably came from Spain and settled in Britain in around 2500 BCE. They got their name because they buried dead bodies with pottery drinking vessels, or beakers. Unlike the Windmill Hill People, the Beaker People buried the dead in small round graves. They marked the graves by building mounds above them called tumuli.

The Beaker people also buried their dead with weapons such as daggers and battle-axes. Experts think they were more warlike than other tribes. They were also successful traders. Beads known to have been made by them have been found as far away as Greece. The beads must have been exported from Britain.

ANCIENT SECRETS

Burial Mounds

In Japan, the Kofun Culture of the third century CE developed an elaborate ritual based on funerals. Little is known about these early Japanese people, but experts know that they built keyhole-shaped burial mounds as tombs for their ruling classes. Kofun is the Japanese word for the burial mounds they built. The mounds varied from a few feet long to over 1300 feet (400 meters) in length.

← This huge keyhole-shaped tomb in Japan stands in the middle of a large lake.

The Wessex People built West Kennet Long Barrow. About 50 people were buried inside.

Like the Windmill Hill People, the Beaker People built earthworks and stone circles. It may be that they built the early part of Stonehenge.

The Wessex People

It is thought that Stonehenge was completed by the Wessex People, who arrived in the Bronze Age, in around 1500 BCE. They built villages at crossroads, which suggests that they traded widely in southwest England.

There is a carving of a bronze dagger on one of the large sarsen stones at Stonehenge. Experts know that the Wessex People used bronze tools and weapons, so they probably made the carving. If the Wessex People did build the second and third stages of Stonehenge, they must have been highly organized and wealthy.

ANCIENT SECRETS

An Ancient Queen

In legends, Stonehenge is often linked with the British heroine Boudicca. Boudicca was queen of the Celtic Iceni people. She led a British uprising against the Romans who invaded Britain. One story is that Boudicca was buried at Stonehenge after her death in battle. Another is that the queen actually built the monument. Evidence at the site shows that neither story is true.

← Some people have suggested that Stonhenge was built by Boudicca, queen of the Iceni people.

How Was Stonehenge Built?

One of the biggest mysteries about Stonehenge is how prehistoric people could have planned and built it. Even getting the giant stones to the site would have been a challenge.

There are many questions about how early builders could have constructed Stonehenge. The answers to some of the questions may never be known. One of the most obvious mysteries is about technology.

No one knows how the builders moved the huge stones into place.

Without iron tools, how were the ancient workers able to carve the stones into shape? Without cranes, how did they pull the 30-ton (27–metric ton) stones upright? Experts know that the ancient Britons had no wheeled vehicles and did not use animals to pull or carry loads. How did they move the huge stones? This last question is the most intriguing of all. This is because scientists now know that the stone used was not quarried locally because of where the stones came from. Builders would have had to move the stones a long way before construction could even begin.

Finding the Stones

Geologists are scientists who study rocks. They look at the chemicals found in a rock to discover where it came from. They tested the chemicals in the sarsen stones at Stonehenge.

Bluetone gets its name
because it looks blue
when it is wet.

The Bluestones
Eighty bluestones stood in two rings inside the monument. Chemical analysis of the rocks shows that they could only have come from one place: the Preseli Hills in Wales. These hills are 135 miles (215 km) away from Stonehenge.

The scientists found that the sarsen stones came from a quarry about 25 miles (40 km) from Stonehenge, near the modern village of Avebury.

The smaller bluestones came from even farther away, in the Preseli Hills of southwest Wales. They must have been transported over 135 miles (215 km) to the site at Stonehenge. But how were the stones moved? And why would the builders have gone to so much effort?

Moving the Stones

People have wondered for centuries how the huge stones were moved to Stonehenge. The largest sarsen stones can weigh up to 30 tons (27 t). They would be difficult to move even with modern technology.

One way archaeologists have tried to solve the mystery is by experimenting. They have tried moving stones themselves. In the 1960s, a British archaeologist named Richard Atkinson suggested that the ancient workers pulled the sarsen stones on wooden **sleds**. He thought they may have used rollers beneath the sled. Atkinson and his young students tested his theory.

The bluestones came from the Preseli Hills in Wales.

↑ Atkinson's reconstruction of how a sled and rollers may have been used to move the stones.

A New Mystery

Thirty-two of Atkinson's students tried moving a stone with a sled and rollers. They managed to drag a 1.5-ton (1.3 t) block about 330 feet (100 m). The largest sarsen stones at Stonehenge were up to 20 times heavier.

From the results of his experiment, Atkinson was able to figure out how much effort it would take to move one of the sarsen stones. He thought it would have taken up to 1,500 workers nine weeks to move one stone from the quarry to Stonehenge. Moving all 81 sarsen stones would have taken at least five years. Atkinson's theory raised another question. Where did all the workers come from? At the time, settlements had few people.

What Came Next?

Atkinson had perhaps answered one question. This led to another. When the stones were at the site, they had to be shaped. The workers set out to make the sides as smooth and regular as possible. How did they do this? Experts at Stonehenge believe they know the answer. They found many stones known as **mauls**. The largest mauls are the size of soccer balls, while the smallest are the size of tennis balls. These mauls were hit against and rubbed over edges and surfaces.

This aerial photograph shows the position and size of the original stone circles.

29

The tenon can clearly be seen sticking up from the top of this upright stone.

The mauls were also used to make the joints to hold the sarsen lintels in place. The builders chipped away at the top of each upright sarsen stone to leave a cone-shaped lump known as a tenon. On the bottom of each lintel they chipped out two hollows known as mortises. When the lintel was placed on top of the upright stones, the tenons slotted into the mortises. This made the structure stable.

If the lintels had simply rested across the top of the uprights, they would have moved. The mortise and tenon joint was one of the earliest carpentry techniques. It is still used by woodworkers today.

How Were the Stones Lifted?

Another mystery remains. How did the workers raise the huge stones into place without using any kind of machines? Experts have many different theories. One suggestion is that the workers first dug a hole in which an upright stone would stand. Using strong tree trunks, they built a large wooden frame shaped like a letter A to stand above the hole.

Builders also lifted huge stones off the ground at other sites in Britain. This is Lanyon Quoit in Cornwall.

Ropes were tied to the stone and then pulled up over the A-frame. This pulled the stone upright until it tipped into the hole.

Another theory is that the workers built a huge ramp by piling up earth. They dragged the stone up the ramp, then pushed it over the end into a hole. No one is sure if that is even possible with such heavy stones.

IN CONTEXT

Solving Ancient Puzzles
Stonehenge is not the only ancient puzzle for experts. In 1970, a crew sailed *Ra II* across the Atlantic Ocean. They built the reed raft based on old drawings from Egypt. Their voyage showed that it was possible that ancient Egyptians had crossed the Atlantic. It did not prove, however, that the Egyptians ever made the crossing.

Experts built *Ra II* and sailed it across the Atlantic Ocean.

↑ How the lintels were raised is one of the most puzzling mysteries.

There is no sign of large amounts of earth having been moved at the site. If this method had been used, where did the earth come from to build the ramps?

A Wooden Frame

It seems unlikely that A-frames or ramps were used to lift the lintels over 20 feet (6.2 m) into the air. Some experts suggest instead that they might have been raised on a platform of heavy logs arranged in crisscross layers, one on top of the other, set at right angles to the layer beneath. Levers could have been used to raise one end of the lintel to slide a new log underneath. Then the other end of the lintel could be raised, and another log added.

SCIENCE SOLVES IT

Moving the Bluestones

At Stonehenge, experts have tried various methods to show how the bluestones might have been moved to the site. One theory is that they were moved from the Preseli Hills in South Wales to Stonehenge by boat. However, when a specially made raft attempted to make the journey in 2003, the raft sank and the stone sank to the bottom of the sea!

Working in this way would raise the lintels a few inches at a time. It would have been a very slow process to raise each lintel to the height needed to then place it across the top of the standing stones.

There is no definite answer as to how this was done. The stones are so heavy it seems almost impossible that they were moved without the use of advanced tools. All that is known for certain is that they were moved—because many are still standing today.

The carefully shaped blocks at Stonehenge fit together tightly.

↑ Modern archaeologists live in reconstructions of Iron Age homes to find out what life was like.

Experimental Archaeology

How Stonehenge was built remains a mystery. The most likely way it will be solved is through **experimental archaeology**. This is when experts try to reconstruct the past by using the same tools and materials used by ancient people. This might mean melting iron as people did in the Iron Age. The experiments do not always work. When experts tried to make Roman cement, the wall they built collapsed in the rain—but they figured it out in the end. Perhaps if people try building a Stonehenge for themselves, they will finally figure out exactly how the ancient builders did it.

Why Did People Build Stone Circles?

Stonehenge is just one of thousands of stone monuments. Can other standing stones reveal the mystery of why they were built?

Stonehenge is not the only ancient stone monument. In different parts of Britain and Europe, groups of ancient people went to great efforts to place huge stones in special arrangements. One kind of arrangement is **dolmen**. This is a sort of chamber made from a flat stone forming a roof across two or more upright stones.

Another common arrangement is a simple stone circle. For this, a number of stones are set upright to form a regular circle. The stones that form this type of monument are called **megaliths**. Sometimes, a megalith was simply set up on its own, not as part of a larger structure.

Callanish Stone Circle was built in Scotland between 2900 and 2600 BCE. ↑

36

↑ The Heel Stone stands on its own outside the main stone circles at Stonehenge.

The Henges

Circular earthworks like the one at Stonehenge are called "henges." They were usually outlined by a circular ditch with a bank on its edge or inside it. There was at least one gap left in the ditch to form an entrance. Experts do not know exactly what this entrance was for. They think it may be connected with a henge's sacred purpose. At Stonehenge, they have found filled-in pits, **postholes**, burial mounds, and standing stones. These suggest that the site was used for special ceremonies—but no one knows what they were.

Was Stonehenge a Burial Site?

Many experts now believe that Stonehenge may have been a memorial for the dead. There are a few human burials scattered around the monument. Some of the holes that were dug into the bank inside the circular ditch and then filled in again also contain ashes from burned human remains. Two stones called the "Station Stones" stand on mounds called barrows. Usually barrows were built over tombs, but these barrows are empty. They do not contain any clues about why they were built.

The Heel Stone may have been used as a guide to line up the main stones with the sunrise.

Experts have suggested that Stonehenge might have been the final place of a funeral journey. They have studied the location of sacred sites in the area.

↑ The stones at Carnac stand in parallel rows that stretch for about half a mile (800 m).

They say that mourners in a funeral procession could have followed a route from the Avon River past the sacred sites to reach Stonehenge by sunset. The only evidence that supports this theory is the location of the sites. But their positions may be completely random. It is not even known if the ancient Britons thought any of the sacred sites had any spiritual connection with one another.

ANCIENT SECRETS

The Carnac Stones

Carnac in northwest France has more than 3,000 standing stones in rows, circles, and fans. Who built them? And did they build nearby prehistoric mounds, called tumuli, to bury their dead? Carnac also has burial chambers known as dolmens. These were made by placing a flat stone on several vertical stones. The stones were enclosed by a mound, but over time the earth has disappeared.

↑ Modern concrete plugs show where stones are now missing from the circle at Avebury.

Careful Alignment

Whatever ceremonies took place at Stonehenge, it is known they were linked to the movements of the sun. The sun rises at different points on the horizon during the year. The stones at Stonehenge are aligned precisely according to the position of the sun on the longest and shortest days of the year.

On the summer solstice, which is midsummer's day and the longest day of the year, the sun at Stonehenge rises directly above the Heel Stone. As the sun's first rays hit the stone circle, they pierce straight to its center, between the two arms of the horseshoe of sarsen stones. On the winter solstice, midwinter's day and the shortest day of the year, the sun sets directly opposite the Heel Stone. The stones are precisely aligned with the position of the sun. The builders clearly positioned them for that purpose.

Other Megaliths

What about the other stone monuments? Experts still do not know how Stonehenge is related to other megaliths in the area. Could the nearby stone circles at Avebury have been part of the whole Stonehenge complex?

The henge at Avebury is just 15 miles (25 km) north of Stonehenge. It was once one of Europe's largest henges. It had several rings of sarsen stones inside a circular ditch, but many of the stones are now missing.

ANCIENT SECRETS

The Biggest Stone

At Locmariaquer in Brittany, France, builders set up the largest standing stone ever known in around 4700 BCE. It stood 65 feet (20 m) tall. About 700 years after it was put up, however, the stone fell and broke. Today it still lies in pieces. It is known in French as Le Grande Menhir Brisé ("brisé" means "broken"). No one knows who erected the menhir or what its purpose was. The complete stone was so heavy that modern engineers have no real idea how ancient peoples moved it around.

Le Grande Menhir Brisé still lies in pieces where it fell in around 4000 BCE.

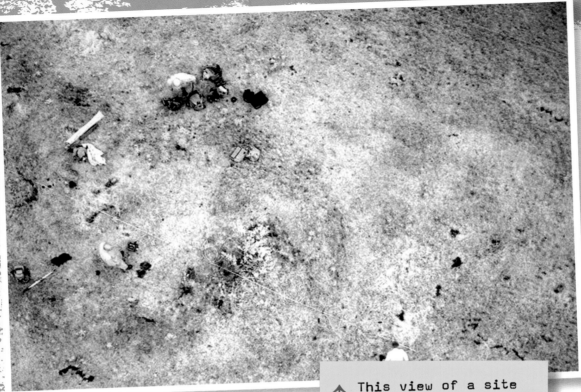

↑ This view of a site in Scotland shows how aerial photographs reveal uneven areas in the land surface.

SCIENCE SOLVES IT

Looking Down!

Since the early 1900s, experts have used aerial photography to study archaeological sites. From above, it is sometimes possible to see outlines in the ground that are not visible at ground level. In 1906, Stonehenge became one of the first sites to be pictured from the air, when photographs were taken from a balloon. Today, aerial photography is invaluable in helping experts locate new sites.

The missing stones at Avebury left holes in the ground. Today, the holes are marked by concrete posts to help indicate the size of the original stone rings. Historians think that the missing stones may have been taken to build local houses. There is little naturally occurring stone near Avebury village—and quite a few houses there are made from stone!

Giant Stones

Perhaps Stonehenge may be related to other stone monuments. In Britain, stone circles were built as far north as Scotland and as far south as Cornwall. As at Stonehenge and Avebury, these stones were always placed in circles. In other places in Europe, however, stones were arranged in circles but also in rows or dolmens. Sometimes, extremely large stones were erected on their own. This was common practice in northwest France.

IN CONTEXT

A Wood Henge

In 1925, aerial photographs revealed a circle of depressions in the ground at Durrington Walls, near Stonehenge. Experts believe they were holes for wooden posts. Their circular layout was similar to the layout of stones at Stonehenge. Were the two sites linked? No one is sure, but Woodhenge, as the site is known, might have been a wooden echo of the stone monument.

These logs mark the position of an ancient wooded circle at Durrington Walls.

This stone circle was built at Castlerigg in northwest England in about 3200 BCE.

IN CONTEXT

Stone Circles

About 1,300 stone circles still stand in Britain and Brittany. The earliest examples date from around 5000 BCE. The monuments vary in size from Stonehenge to smaller circles where moving the stones would have been quite easy. There is no sign of anyone living at a stone circle, and very few of the circles are associated with graves or burials. Experts think they must have been used for some kind of ceremonies. What those ceremonies were, however, remains a mystery.

Brittany is home to many single stones, as well as the stone lines at Carnac. These sites raise as many questions as Stonehenge itself. What were the Carnac stones for? How did the builders erect the massive stone at Locmariaquer? Although it has fallen over, the mystery remains of how it was put up in the first place. Even modern cranes would not have been able to lift its 350-ton (320 t) weight.

Who Built the Megaliths?

It may be that we will never know why or how people built the standing stones. Many experts have tried to explain the purpose of Stonehenge. None of their theories have been accepted by everyone. Each piece of new evidence raises new questions. In the early 1900s, many people believed the megaliths were inspired by Mycenae in ancient Greece. The Mycenaeans were known for building megalithic monuments. In the 1960s, however, radiocarbon dating proved that the megaliths in Europe were much older than those in Mycenae.

The mystery remains unsolved. The archaeologist Richard Atkinson once said, "Most of what has been written about Stonehenge is nonsense or **speculation**. No one will ever have a clue what its significance was."

It is known that Stonehenge was linked to the movement of the sun. Why remains a mystery.

Glossary

archaeologists People who study the past by examining old ruins, objects, and records.

belief system The ideas a group of people use to explain their world and their lives.

carbon A chemical present in all living things.

ceremonial Describes something used in solemn rituals or ceremonies.

dolmen A tomb formed by a large flat stone placed on top of a number of upright stones.

druid A priest of the ancient Celts, or a modern follower of a nature-based religion.

earthworks Large banks of soil that were often built for defense.

enclosures Areas surrounded by earthworks.

experimental archaeology A form of archaeology in which people learn about the past by trying to re-create past conditions.

mauls Ball-shaped hammers made from rocks.

megaliths Large stones in prehistoric monuments.

plateau A flat area of raised ground.

postholes Holes cut into the earth to hold posts of wood or stone.

rituals Religious ceremonies in which actions take place in a set manner and order.

sacred Connected with a god or gods, and therefore deserving of worship.

sacrifices Offerings made to the gods, including by killing animals or even humans.

semi-nomadic Describes people who split their time between living in settlements and roaming in search of food.

sleds Vehicles with runners that are pulled over snow or other surfaces.

solstice Either the longest or shortest days of the year.

speculation Describes a theory or conclusion that is not based on firm evidence.

spiritual Relating to sacred or religious matters.

standing stones Stones that have deliberately been set upright in the ground.

symmetrical Having a shape in which one part reflects another.

theories Ideas that try to explain something that is not known for certain.

volcanic Produced by a volcano.

Further Resources

Books

Aronson, Marc. *If Stones Could Speak: Unlocking the Secrets of Stonehenge.* Washington, DC: National Geographic Children's Books, 2010.

Capek, Michael. *Stonehenge.* Digging Up the Past. Minneapolis, MN: Essential Library, 2014.

Kelley, True. *Where Is Stonehenge.* Where Is? New York: Turtleback, 2016.

McDaniel, Sean. *Stonehenge.* The Unexplained. Minneapolis, MN: Bellwether Media, 2011.

Owings, Lisa. *Stonehenge.* Unexplained Mysteries. Minneapolis, MN: Bellwether Media, 2014.

Sabatino, Michael. *20 Fun Facts About Stonehenge.* Fun Fact File: World Wonders. New York: Gareth Stevens Publishing, 2014.

Websites

http://www.bbc.co.uk/guides/zg8q2hv
This Bitesize guide from the BBC history site has videos and graphics about Stonehenge.

http://www.coolfactsforkids.com/ stonehenge-facts-for-kids/
This page has a whole range of fascinating facts we known about the monument—and some that we know are not true.

http://www.english-heritage.org.uk/visit/ places/stonehenge/schools/education- film/#
English Heritage, who run Stonehenge today, have made this special educational video for kids.

http://www.fun-facts.org.uk/wonders_of_ world/stonehenge.htm
This British site features 15 fun facts about Stonehenge and has a link to a video about the world's ancient wonders.

http://www.softschools.com/facts/ wonders_of_the_world/stonehenge_ facts/92/
This page from Softschools.com has interesting facts about Stonehenge and other wonders of the world.

Publisher's note to educators and parents: Our editors have carefully reviewed these websites to ensure that they are suitable for students. Many websites change frequently, however, and we cannot guarantee that a site's future contents will continue to meet our high standards of quality and educational value. Be advised that students should be closely supervised whenever they access the Internet.

Index

A

aerial photography 42
aliens 6, 7
altar stone 12
antlers 9, 10
Atkinson, Richard 27, 28, 29, 45
Atlantis 6, 7
Aubrey, John 15, 16
Avebury 25, 26, 40, 41, 42, 43
Avon River 12, 39

B

barrows 38
Beaker People 19, 20, 21, 22
bluestones 10, 12, 26, 34
Boudicca 23
Brittany 44
burials 17, 19, 20–21, 38

C

Carnac 39, 44
Celts 14, 15, 16, 23
Chacoan people 11
Cornwall 31, 43

D

dating, radiocarbon 8, 9, 16
ditch, circular 9, 10, 18, 38
dolmen 36, 43
druids 4, 16
Durrington Walls 5, 43

E

earthworks 5, 18, 19, 20, 22, 37
Easter Island 6, 7
Egyptians 7, 14, 15, 32

enclosures 9, 18
experimental archaeology 32, 35

F

Fajada Butte 11
farmers 4, 6, 17, 18
France 39, 41, 43

G H

Grand Menhir Brisé, Le 41
Heel Stone 12, 37, 38, 40
henges 37, 41, 43
Hopewell 20

I J K

Iron Age 5, 35
Japan 21
Kofun Culture 21

L

Lanyon Quoit 31
lintels 8, 30, 31, 33, 34
Locmariaquer 41, 44

M

mauls 29, 30
megaliths 36, 41, 45
menhirs 41
Midsummer's Day see solstice, summer
Mississippian Culture 20
mortise and tenon 30, 31
Mycenae 45

N P

New Stone Age 17
Preseli Hills 26, 27, 34
pyramids 7, 15

R

Ra II 32
radiocarbon dating 8, 16
Romans 14, 15

S

sacrifices 12
Salisbury Plain 5, 19
sarsen stones 11, 12, 23, 25–26, 27, 28
Saxons 7, 8
Slaughter Stone 12
sleds 27, 28
solstice, summer 4, 6, 10, 11, 12, 13, 20, 40
solstice, winter 12, 13, 20, 40
Station Stones 38
stone circles 5, 15, 22, 36, 43, 44
Stonehenge I 10, 18
Stonehenge II 10, 13
Stonehenge III 11
Stonehenge, name 7
Stonehenge, reconstruction 13

T

tools 9, 10, 25
trade 21
tumuli 21, 39

W

Wessex People 19, 22, 23
Windmill Hill 18, 19